THEMATIC UNIT
Native Americans

Written by Daphne Ransom

Teacher Created Resources, Inc.
6421 Industry Way
Westminster, CA 92683
www.teachercreated.com

©2000 Teacher Created Resources, Inc.
Reprinted, 2004
Made in U.S.A.

ISBN-1-57690-581-0

Illustrated by
Ken Tunell

Edited by
Janet A. Hale, M.S. Ed.

Cover Art by
Denice Adorno

Table of Contents

Introduction

Native Americans is a captivating 80-page thematic unit filled with a wide variety of lesson ideas and activities designed for young children. For each of the four featured books—*Native Americans, Little Star, The Goat in the Rug,* and *How Jackrabbit Got His Very Long Ears*—activities are included that set the stage for reading, encourage the enjoyment of the book, and extend the concepts gained. In addition, the theme is connected to the curriculum using activities in language arts (including language experience and writing suggestions), math, science, art, music, and life skills (cooking, physical education, etc.). Many of the included activities encourage cooperative learning. Suggestions and patterns for bulletin boards and learning center activities are time savers for busy teachers. Furthermore, directions are given for a culminating activity, which allows the children to synthesize their knowledge by creating products that can be shared beyond the classroom.

This thematic unit includes the following:

❑ **literature selections**—summaries of three children's books and one booklet with related lessons (complete with reproducible pages) that cross the curriculum

❑ **planning guides**—suggestions for sequencing lessons for each day of the unit

❑ **language experience and writing ideas**—for activities that cross the curriculum

❑ **bulletin-board ideas**—plans for student-created and/or interactive bulletin boards

❑ **curriculum connections**—activities in language arts, math, science, art, music, social studies, physical education, and cooking

❑ **group projects**—projects to foster cooperative learning

❑ **culminating activity**—designed to be a celebration that requires your children to synthesize their learning

❑ **a bibliography**—additional fiction and nonfiction literature based on the theme

---

To keep this valuable resource intact so it can be used year after year, you may wish to punch holes in the pages and store them in a three-ring binder.

Introduction *(cont.)*

Why a Balanced Approach?

The strength of a balanced language approach is that it involves children in using all modes of communication—reading, writing, listening, illustrating, and doing. Communication skills are interconnected and integrated into lessons that emphasize the whole of language. Implicit in this approach is our knowledge that every whole—including individual words—is composed of parts, and directed study of those parts can help a child to master the whole. Experience and research tell us that regular attention to phonics, other word-attack skills, spelling, etc., develops reading mastery, thereby fulfilling the unity of the whole language experience. The child is thus led to read, write, spell, speak, and listen confidently in response to a literature experience introduced by the teacher. In these ways, language skills grow rapidly, stimulated by direct practice, involvement, and interest in the topic at hand.

Why Thematic Planning?

One very useful tool for implementing a balanced language program is thematic planning. By choosing a theme with correlating literature selections for a unit of study, a teacher can plan activities throughout the day that lead to a cohesive, in-depth study of the topic. Children will be practicing and applying their skills in meaningful contexts. Consequently, they will learn and retain more. Both teachers and children will also be freed from a day that is broken into unrelated segments of isolated drill and practice.

Why Cooperative Learning?

Along with academic skills and content, children also need to learn social skills. No longer can this area of development be taken for granted. Children must learn to work cooperatively in groups in order to function well in modern society. Group activities should be a regular part of school life, and teachers should consciously include social objectives as well as academic objectives in their planning. For example, a group working together to write a report may need to select a leader. The teacher should make this clear to the children and monitor the qualities of good leader-follower group interactions just as he or she would state and monitor the academic goals of the project.

Why Journals?

Each day your children should have the opportunity to write in a journal. They may respond to a book or an event in history, write about a personal experience, or answer a general "question of the day" posed by the teacher. Cumulative journals provide an excellent means of documenting children's writing progress.

Native Americans Mini-book

by Daphne Ransom

Summary

This booklet is designed to help your children build an awareness of the first Americans in North America. Though each tribe was/is unique, there are shared similarities such as food, shelter, clothing, communication skills, etc. This booklet includes these similarities and cultivates sensitivity towards Native Americans past and present. Its repetitive dialogue enhances word-recognition skills and makes it enjoyable for a young reader.

The outline below is a suggested plan. You can adapt these ideas and activities to fit your classroom situation.

Sample Plan

Lesson 1

- Introduce the *Native Americans* mini-book (page 6, Setting the Stage, #7).
- Read the "homes" section (the first five pages). Discuss Native-American homes (page 6, Enjoying the Book, #1).
- Assign the matching activity (page 59).
- Sing "Special Homes" (page 68).
- Complete the tepee activity (page 7, Enjoying the Book, #2).

Lesson 2

- Review the "homes" section and read the "food" section of the booklet.
- Discuss foods and growing crops (page 7, #3).
- Complete "Corn-y Plants" (page 66).
- Create a class rain dance (page 69).

Lesson 3

- Review the first two sections of the book and then read the "jobs" section.
- Sing "Native-American Life" (page 68).
- Make a work graph (page 7, #4).

Lesson 4

- Review the first three sections of the booklet and then read the "communication" section.
- Discuss some Native American writing symbols and write symbol messages (page 8, #5).
- Assign a family activity (page 9, #6).

Lesson 5

- Review the first four sections of the booklet and then read the "children" section.
- Discuss the children's jobs (page 7, #4).
- Play Stick-in-the-Hoop and Coup Tag (page 71).

Lesson 6

- Re-read the entire booklet and review the concepts learned.
- Sing "Special Homes" (page 68).
- Create a tepee village (page 9, #7).

Overview of Activities

Setting the Stage

1. To prepare your room, decorate your walls with a bulletin-board display (page 76).

2. Using the bibliography (page 80), collect Native-American resource books. Create a free-time reading corner (page 77, Activity Centers, #1).

3. If desired, you may want to purchase a book from the series *If You Lived with the . . .* (bibliography, page 80), choosing the book that tells of the Native Americans who lived/live in your region of the country. These books are very informative and are written in a question/answer format.

4. Create one or more of the activity centers described on page 77.

5. Reproduce the *Native Americans* Mini-book (pages 10–21), one per child. To assemble, cut the pages apart on the outer bold lines; stack in page-number sequence starting with the title page; and staple along the left-side edge. (Note: Assemble and color one book to be used in the Setting the Stage, #7 activity below.)

6. If possible, obtain photographs or illustrations from your school or local library showing Native-American homes, clothing, and crafts.

7. Gather the children together and show them the pre-made mini-book. Read the title. Explain to them that the Native Americans were the first people to live in North America. Using a globe or map, show the children where North America is and explain to them that the early Native Americans didn't live just in one area of the country. Discuss how the first Americans lived in groups, called tribes, all across North America. Although each tribe was unique, they all had similarities (clothing, food, shelter, etc.). Tell the children that they are going to be learning about the Native Americans of long ago and today.

Enjoying the Book

1. Over a period of several days, read the mini-book to or with your children. The mini-book has been written in sections to make it easier to focus in on one concept for each lesson. Here is a list of possible questions and dialogue that may be used after reading the "homes" section in the mini-book: *What is a home? Who lives in a home? Do all homes look the same? What are homes made from?* Just like us, the first Americans needed a place to live. Their homes were made from materials that they could easily find in their environment.

　　　　6

Overview of Activities (cont.)

Enjoying the Book (cont.)

The longhouse was made using a wood frame covered with bark. The tepee was made using a wood frame as well, although it was covered with buffalo hides. Hogans were lodges made of wood planks covered with thatch (dried grass and reeds). The grass and reeds were then covered with a layer of turf.

After your discussion time on Native-American homes, have the children complete the activity on page 59.

2. Native Americans of the Plains lived in tepees. The majority of them were not farmers. Most of their lives centered on the hunt for buffalo. A tepee could be staked out, raised up, and taken down quickly, enabling them to follow the massive beasts. The tepee frame was made by lacing together eight 20' (6 m) long cedar or pine poles at one end to form a cone shape. The tepee was approximately 15' (4.5 m) in height when the poles were stood up vertically. Using this second measurement, create a two-dimensional tepee display from brown bulletin-board paper. Cut the paper in a triangular fashion with the highest point (top angle) measuring 15' (4.5 m). If desired, have the children decorate the tepee's buffalo skins using Native-American symbols (page 51). Display the tepee on a classroom wall or in the hallway. Brainstorm with the children: *What things are taller than the tepee's height? What things are shorter than the tepee's height?* Write these ideas on two separate sheets of chart paper; display next to the tepee. Follow up this activity using the mathematical sheet on page 57. For this activity, have the students color the tepee. Next, an appropriate illustration needs to be drawn on the left and right sides of the tepee. Have the children color the two added illustrations. For a unique display, fold a completed sheet in thirds; tape the two ends together (The illustrations should be facing out.); and stand up the prism on a table or countertop. (Note: You may want to share with your children the fact that the women were responsible for putting up the tepee poles and covering them with buffalo hides. It took approximately 20 buffalo hides sewn together to cover one tepee frame.)

3. Corn was a main food source for most Native Americans. Both whole-kernel corn and cornmeal were used. *Corn Is Maize* (Bibliography, page 80) is an informational book on how corn was raised and used by Native Americans. Discuss with the children the parts of a corn plant and what it needs to grow. You may want to make a learning center to enhance their learning (Activity Centers, page 77, #5). Reproduce page 66, one for each child, to reinforce the introduced plant vocabulary.

4. Work was an important part of everyday life for the early Native Americans. Everyone in the tribe had jobs. Men made tools and weapons, carved bowls and cups, and made boats and musical instruments. The women made clay pottery, wove baskets and rugs, sewed clothing, and did the gathering and farming of food. Planting, gathering, hunting, and the storing of food took most of their time during the spring, summer, and fall seasons. Winter was spent indoors, making and repairing clothing, tools, and baskets. Make a graph with the children. Ask them what jobs they have to do at home; list the jobs on chart paper. Ask if the jobs are ones they must do year-round, or if the jobs are only done during certain seasons. Create a graph representing the jobs and the seasons the jobs are completed in.

Overview of Activities (cont.)

Enjoying the Book (cont.)

5. Children will love writing their own message using universal picture symbols (page 51). Enlarge/copy this page onto display paper and hang it in your room. (Note: One alternative would be to simply write the symbols on your chalkboard.) These symbols were used to record events, tell stories, and make designs on tepees and clothing. Reproduce page 52 onto brown construction paper, one sheet per child. Have each student cut out the bear shape. (Note: The bear can be optionally "cut out" by making small tears with your fingers around the shape to make it appear rustic.) The children then use their crayons to draw their desired symbols on their bearskins. (Remember, the goal is to have the children create actual messages rather than simply draw a scattering of symbols.) If desired, have the children crumple up their completed bearskin and re-open it to make it look even more like a leathery skin covering.

6. Early Native-American children had jobs but also found time to play. Play one or more of the games listed on pages 69–71.

Extending the Book

1. Before conducting this cornmeal-making activity, gather two stones for grinding—a larger, flat, washed rock (with a little hollow in its center, if possible) for the base stone, and a smaller, flat, washed rock for use as a grinder. You will also need some dried corn on the cob, a package of cornmeal, and a medium-sized container filled with water. Discuss how we get cornmeal today (i.e., at the grocery store). Show them some cornmeal, allowing them to touch it, while discussing how the Native Americans made their cornmeal long ago. Show the corn on the cob. Provide each child with three or four kernels (remove the kernels from the cob). Ask them to look at the kernels closely and share anything they may notice or discover. Soak the kernels in the bowl of water overnight. Drain off the water the next morning; dry off any excess water with a paper towel. Allow the children to take turns grinding the corn by placing a small amount of the kernels in the center of the larger stone and pressing downward on the pieces using the smaller stone. The goal is to crush the pieces into small particles (meal).

2. Make a class big book. Enlarge the bear-skin pattern (page 52) onto two sheets of tagboard (front and back covers). Provide each child with a sheet of chart paper that has the same dimensions as the tagboard sheets. Using Native-American writing symbols (page 51), have each child write his/her own message on the paper. Assemble the pages and covers; bind. Place the big book in your reading area (page 6, #2). Children will enjoy reading each other's symbolic sentences.

Overview of Activities (cont.)

Extending the Book (cont.)

3. Reproduce page 62, one per child. Teach or review the numerals 1–10. Have them connect the dots to complete the Pueblo dwelling. As a variation, make lacing cards by gluing copies of page 62 onto tagboard; laminate and cut around the pattern, leaving a small border. Punch a hole at each number. Provide shoelaces or yarn for lacing. (Note: If using yarn, dip one end of the yarn in clear nail polish or wax to prevent fraying.)

4. Many Native-American tribes spoke different languages. Oftentimes when two different tribes met, they would use sign language to communicate. Teach some simple signs that can be reinforced throughout the unit. You may want to enlarge pages 49–50 to be placed as a poster in a dramatic-play area.

5. Rain was essential to the tribes for helping their crops grow and nourishing themselves, their livestock, and the nearby wild game. Rain dances were often performed in times of drought. Create a rain dance (page 69) and add rhythm sounds using instruments made by the children (page 78).

6. Send a copy of page 54 home with each child. Each child completes the front by circling the correct Native-American symbol and by drawing their own symbolic pictures where indicated. The rest of the family then draws information about themselves on the back side of the sheet. Display the family pictures when returned.

7. Create a Plains tepee village. Each child will need one-half of a 6" (15 cm) soft tortilla shell, colored markers, four small pretzel sticks, a toothpick, and some canned frosting. To create a tepee, use the colored markers to decorate one side of the tortilla half. Roll the decorated tortilla into a cone shape and prick a toothpick through both layers to hold the cone in place. Place a small amount of frosting inside the cone near its tip. Place four pretzels inside the cone, gently pressing against the frosting to form the tepee's frame.

To create a tepee village, first use some blue paint to create a river on a small section of green bulletin-board paper. Set the finished tepees in small circular groups on the green paper near the painted river. In the center of each ring of tepees, make a small circle of pebbles to represent a fire ring. Add broken-up pretzel sticks in the middle of each fire ring to represent wood.

Native Americans **Mini-book**

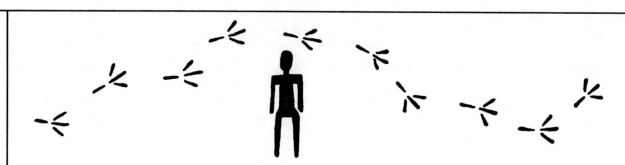

Some Native Americans lived in tepees.

1

Native Americans **Mini-book** *(cont.)*

Some Native Americans lived in longhouses.

2

Some Native Americans lived in Pueblo dwellings.

3

Native Americans Mini-book *(cont.)*

Some Native Americans lived in hogans.   **4**

But today, Native Americans live in houses a lot like mine.   **5**

Native Americans **Mini-book** *(cont.)*

Some Native Americans hunted with bows and arrows. 6

Some Native Americans fished for food. 7

Native Americans **Mini-book** *(cont.)*

Some Native Americans gathered nuts and berries.　　**8**

Some Native Americans planted corn, pumpkins, and beans.　**9**

Native Americans **Mini-book** *(cont.)*

But today, Native Americans get their food the same way I do. 10

Some Native Americans made tools and weapons. **11**

Native Americans **Mini-book** *(cont.)*

Some Native Americans made baskets and pottery.　12

Some Native Americans wove rugs and blankets.　13

Native Americans **Mini-book** (cont.)

Some Native Americans made clothing.

14

But today, Native Americans have jobs
just like my family does.

15

Native Americans **Mini-book** *(cont.)*

Some Native Americans used sign language.   16

Some Native Americans used smoke signals.   17

Native Americans **Mini-book** *(cont.)*

Some Native Americans wrote stories using pictures. **18**

But today, Native Americans talk to each other just like my friends and I do. **19**

Native Americans **Mini-book** *(cont.)*

Some Native American children played with straw dolls.   **20**

Some Native American children pretended to be warriors.   **21**

Native Americans Mini-book (cont.)

**All Native American children played games and learned
about the world around them.**

22

**Today, Native American children play and go to school
just like I do.**

23

Little Star

by Mary Packard

Summary

Little Star, named after the Great Star spirit who had blessed her birth, used a special wish her father granted her to help a favorite horse get well instead of using the wish for her own happiness. Little Star *is heart-touching story of selflessness and patience that all will enjoy.*

The outline below is a suggested plan. You can adapt these ideas and activities to fit your classroom situation.

Sample Plan

Lesson 1

- Teach some of the story's vocabulary (page 23, Setting the Stage, #2).

- Read *Little Star*.

- Sing "Little Star" (page 68).

- Create Little Star's necklace (page 24, Enjoying the Book, #6).

- Send home naming notes (page 23, Setting the Stage, #1).

Lesson 2

- Reread *Little Star* and sing "Little Star" (page 68).

- Complete the maze activity (page 23, Enjoying the Book, #1).

- Create a Native-American vest (page 24, Extending the Book, #6).

Lesson 3

- Review the story.

- Make drums (page 78) and enjoy a syllabication activity to reinforce the story's vocabulary (page 24, Extending the Book, #5).

- Draw horses (page 24, Enjoying the Book, #4).

- Build fine-motor skills using pegboards (page 23, Enjoying the Book, #2).

Lesson 4

- Play vocabulary-oriented "Go Fish" (page 24, #2).

- Complete an initial-consonant activity (page 53).

- Review Native-American clothing and play a hide-and-seek game (page 23, #3).

- Complete the moccasin-matching activity (page 24, #1).

Overview of Activities

Setting the Stage

1. Native-American children were named after animals, plants, or a natural occurrence that happened during or soon after their birth. With your children, make a list on chart paper of the characters in the upcoming story. Have them think of why each name was given; list their ideas next to that character's name. Send home the naming note (page 79) asking the parents to share a "special event" of his/her child's birth (late at night, snowing outside, etc.). When the children return with the information, create a Native-American name for each child and write each name on a piece of white construction paper. Have each child then illustrate his/her special name's event.

2. Teach some vocabulary words that will help your children understand *Little Star* better. Explain to them that they will be "gigging." Gigging is catching fish by dragging a hook through a school of fish. Reproduce the picture cards (pages 25–26) onto tagboard. Cut out the fish shapes; laminate, if desired. Attach a paper clip to each fish near its face. Tie a string to the end of a 36" (91 cm) stick for use as a fishing pole. Tie a washer-shaped magnet to the other end of the string. Have the children take turns gigging a fish. Discuss each picture and vocabulary word as it is caught. Display the fish cards or place the cards and pole in a learning center area.

Enjoying the Book

1. Show the cover of *Little Star*. Ask the children what they think the story may be about. Begin reading; periodically stop to ask appropriate questions, such as: *What does Little Star love most of all? What does her father feel she needs to learn to do?* Ask the children if they have ever wanted something so much they could hardly stand waiting. *What was it? Did their parents make them wait to get it? Why? Is it hard to wait?* Have the children complete the maze activity (page 28).

2. Set out pegboards during free-exploration time to work on fine-motor skills. Children can copy the pegboard pattern found on page 27. (An alternative to using pegboards is to provide graphing paper and have the children color in the dotted squares to form the horse.)

3. Slowly page through the book, taking time to look at the clothing worn by Little Star and her family. Discuss the names of the clothing (leggings, dress, vest, moccasins, etc.). At one time, clothing was made primarily from animal skins, and most items were adorned with beautiful bead work and porcupine quills. Play "Moccasin," a Native-American guessing game with your children. You will need four slippers and a stone. While the children cover their eyes, hide the stone in one of the slippers. Let the children now guess where the stone is hidden. They will enjoy making their own paper guessing game by coloring and cutting out the stone and moccasins found on page 70.

Overview of Activities *(cont.)*

Enjoying the Book *(cont.)*

4. Little Star wanted a horse more than anything. When she used her special wish to help the mare, the colt was born with a star shape on its forehead. Have the children try to draw their own horses (page 29) and name them.

5. Seat the children on the floor with the girls and boys facing each other. Teach and sing the song "Little Star" (page 68), adding your own motions to the words.

6. Allow the children to create Little Star's necklace (like the one included with the purchase of the book) using a dough recipe (page 67). Give each child a small amount of dough. The dough needs to be rolled into a ball, then flattened into a disk shape. Make two holes side-by-side at the top of the disk using a thin drinking straw. When the disk is dry, supply tempera paints and have each child decorate his/her disk to resemble the star shape on Little Star's necklace. Weave a piece of yarn through the holes to form the necklace. (Note: You may want to keep these at school for the children to wear during the culminating activities [page 74].)

Extending the Book

1. After discussing Native-American clothing with your children, make one copy of page 60 for each child. Have the children complete this activity by looking at the moccasin in the left box and finding its mate in the corresponding row.

2. Play "Go Fish" by first reproducing two sets of fish cards (pages 25–26) on tagboard. Color, cut out, and laminate the fish cards. Explain to the children that this fish game is played in the same way as the traditional "Go Fish" game. For an extension, you can use the cards to play a traditional concentration game for one or two players.

3. Teach or review the numerals 1–6. Practice counting objects in the room that represent sets of one to six. Have the children complete a counting worksheet (page 55).

4. Once the children have become familiar with many of the new vocabulary words introduced in this story, reinforce their initial consonant-sound skills by completing page 53.

5. Breaking down whole words into sound parts is an important beginning-reading skill. The children will love this simple syllabication activity. Make a drum (page 78). Then, using the words from pages 25–26 along with any others you choose from the story, have the children take turns tapping out the syllables of each word on the drum.

6. Many Native Americans wore vests made from animal skins. Create vests (page 67) for your children to wear. You may want to make two or three extra vests to be used in a dramatic-play area. You may also want your children to wear their vests during the unit's culminating activities (page 74).

7. When purchasing the *Little Star* book, you also receive a beaded star necklace. Choose one child per day to be your special Little Star (line leader, paper monitor, etc.) and have that child wear Little Star's beaded necklace for the day.

8. If possible, visit a museum that has Native-American artifacts and paintings.

Go Fish

Go Fish *(cont.)*

canoe

dress

horse

basket

arrow

saddle

blanket

Pegboard Horse

Where's My Horse?

Lead Little Star to her horse.

28

How to Draw a Horse

Draw your own horse.

The Goat in the Rug

by Charles L. Blood and Martin Link

Summary

The Goat in the Rug is a charming, true story about a Navajo weaver who decides to weave her friend, Geraldine the goat—or rather, her wool—into a rug. The step-by-step process of making a rug is told through the eyes of the goat. This book shows the close friendship between Geraldine and Glenmae and also that it takes cooperation to get a job done.

The outline below is a suggested plan. You can adapt these ideas and activities to fit your classroom situation.

Sample Plan

Lesson 1

- Examine and discuss natural materials (page 31, Setting the Stage, #1).
- Discuss and demonstrate, or have your children try, weaving on a loom (page 31, Enjoying the Book, #2).
- Read *The Goat in the Rug* (page 31, Setting the Stage, #3).
- Discuss soft objects versus hard objects (page 32, #6)
- Sing "Weaving a Rug" (page 68).

Lesson 2

- Reread and sequence the story's events (page 31, #4).
- If possible, touch and feel unprocessed wool (page 31, Enjoying the Book, #3).
- Create a weaver (page 32, #7).
- Sing "Weaving a Rug" (page 68).

Lesson 3

- Discuss the natural-dying process (page 31, Enjoying the Book, #1).
- Complete a coloring activity (page 32, #8).
- Discuss the resourcefulness of the early Native Americans (page 32, #2).
- Geraldine was a great storyteller. Share the two "illustrated" stories found on pages 47 and 48.

Lesson 4

- Review the weaving process; then make woven placemats (page 67).
- Complete the woven-basket activity (page 33).
- Make hogans (page 31, #5).

Overview of Activities

Setting the Stage

1. Set out a number of natural materials for your children to examine, such as tree bark, moss, leaves, stones, shells, clay, sand, wool, leather, bones, etc. Label each item to foster word-recognition skills and to promote writing activities. If feasible, take time to discuss the words that can be used to describe how the materials feel.

2. If possible, obtain a variety of Native-American music and play the music softly in the background as the school day unfolds.

3. Introduce the book by showing the cover and reading the title. Ask the children what they think the story is about. Read *The Goat in the Rug*. When finished, ask these comprehension questions: *Who is telling the story? What is the goat's name? Who is Geraldine's friend? What does Glenmae make? Does it take a long time to make a rug? Is this a true story?*

Enjoying the Book

1. Berries, vegetables, and fruits were, and are, used by many Native Americans for dying fabrics/cloth. Vegetables and fruits that have been cut into small pieces can be rubbed or pounded into already-woven cloth. Provide an area that has been covered with newspaper. Have your children use small remnants of muslin and experiment with a variety of food and plant pieces that they can gently crush into the cloth. Display their finished products.

2. Challenge the children with a weaving activity. Tie or nail four 12" (30 cm) wooden dowels or sticks together to form a square frame. Staple a 13" x 13" (33 cm x 33 cm) piece of burlap to the frame. Cut long, vertical slits into the burlap, approximately 3" (8 cm) apart, leaving approximately 1" (2.54 cm) of material at both the top and bottom of each slit. Set a bag of colored rag or yarn strips beside the frame (loom) and allow time for the children to test their weaving skills.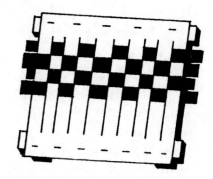

3. Obtain unprocessed wool from a farmer or craft-supply shop. Allow the children to wash and dry the wool. If possible, provide carding combs to comb the wool smooth. Keep a small basket of unprocessed wool and carding combs in the dramatic-play area for free time or planned use.

4. Re-read the story, pausing to discuss the steps in making a rug. Follow the discussion with a sequencing activity (page 35), making one copy of this page for each child. Provide each child with sentence strips, scissors, crayons, and glue. Have the children color and cut apart the squares. Then have them glue the pictures in the correct sequence on the paper strip.

5. Tell the children that you are going to slowly leaf through the pages of the book and you want them to say "stop" when they see Glenmae's home. Discuss what kind of home she lives in (hogan). Make miniature hogans using large Styrofoam cups, brown markers, scissors, small strands of straw or raffia, and glue. Color the cups brown using the markers. Turn the cups upside-down, so their openings are faced down. Cut out a small arched doorway area. Glue small pieces of straw or raffia on the cups' bottoms to form the roofs.

Overview of Activities (cont.)

Enjoying the Book (cont.)

6. Discuss with the children what the wool from a goat or sheep feels like. Is it soft or hard? Brainstorm things that are soft and hard. Write their ideas down on chart paper or simply discuss verbally. Have them complete the classifying activity (page 38) using magazines, scissors, and glue. Have them cut pictures of hard and soft objects from the magazines and glue them under the appropriate heading.

7. Have the children make a weaver portrait. Provide each child with a copy of page 36 reproduced onto tagboard. Each child will need crayons, scissors, glue, an 8" (20 cm) length of yarn, and a brad fastener. First, color and cut out the weaving scene, as well as the Navajo woman's arm. Glue the yarn, in a curled-up fashion, onto the basket, leaving a 4" (10 cm) length of yarn free (do not glue this length down). Attach the right-side arm to the shoulder by pressing a brad fastener first through the arm and then through the shoulder; open up the prongs of the brad fastener. Cut a small slit in the weaver's right hand and place the end of the 4" (10 cm) length in the slit. Move the weaving arm up and down and watch the woman weave her rug.

8. Review the basic color words with your children. Complete the color activity found on page 37. Have them identify each color word and then color the goats appropriately.

Extending the Book

1. Native Americans wove more than just rugs. They wove blankets, sashes, and baskets, too. If possible, show examples of any of these woven items. Reproduce a copy of page 33 for each child and have them complete this fun sheet.

2. The first Native Americans were very resourceful. They used everything in their environment to make the things they needed. Have the children think back to the discussions on Native-American homes (*Native Americans* Mini-book, pages 10–12). Explain to them that when an animal was killed, not only was the hide used to make tepees and clothing and the meat used for eating, but also even the bones were used for such things as sewing needles, jewelry, and special breastplates, worn by warriors. Have the students complete a cut-and-paste activity (page 34). Color and cut apart the four bottom pictures. Match the pictures with their partnered object. Paste the pictures in the correct squares.

3. If possible, ask a farmer to visit your class, or better yet, schedule a field trip to a farm. Ask to see a sheep or goat being sheared.

4. Native Americans are well known for their handcrafted clay pottery. They were/are painted with very intricate, geometric designs, and placed in outdoor ovens for firing. Have the children complete the pottery pattern worksheet (page 58). For an extension activity, have them create a real clay pot. Using the dough recipe (page 67), pinch off a small ball of clay and flatten it into a small disk. Pinch off another small ball of clay and roll it in the palms of your hands to form a "snake." Coil the snake around the perimeter of the disk and continue in an upward fashion to make the sides of the pot. Allow the pot to dry; then paint it with tempera paints. (Note: You may want to keep the pottery in the classroom to display during the culminating activities [page 74]).

5. Today, we have many comforts that the Native Americans of long ago did not have (e.g., telephones, electricity, cars, clocks, television, etc.). Have the children complete page 61.

What's in the Woven Basket?

Color the basket. Draw something in the basket.

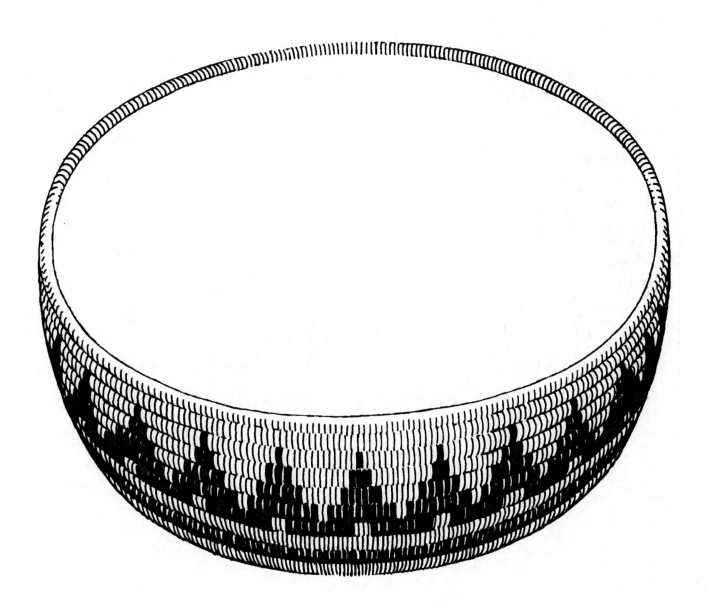

My basket is filled with _____.

What Was I Used For?

buffalo

bones

bark

wool

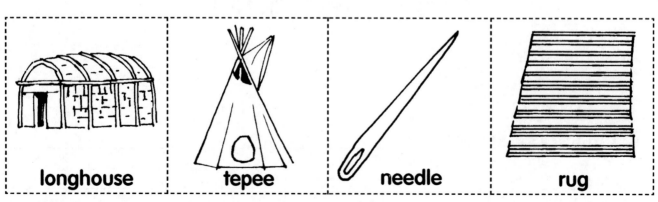

longhouse   tepee   needle   rug

34

Weaving a Rug

Color, cut, and paste in order.

A Weaver

Goats of a Different Color

red

green

blue

orange

yellow

purple

black

brown

white

Soft or Hard?

soft   hard

How Jackrabbit Got His Very Long Ears

by Heather Irbinskas

Summary

This is a story about four animals that make the desert their home. Jackrabbit was chosen by the Great Spirit to lead some desert creatures (a tortoise, a bobcat, and a roadrunner) to their new homes, as well as tell them how special they were made in order to survive in such a hot and barren land. However, Jackrabbit was not a good listener when the Great Spirit was telling him about the uniqueness of each creature and feelings got hurt. This is a sensitive story that teaches children to listen carefully and to treat others kindly.

The outline below is a suggested plan. You can adapt these ideas and activities to fit your classroom situation.

Sample Plan

Lesson 1

- If possible, make animal-track reliefs (page 40, Setting the Stage, #1).
- Read *How Jackrabbit Got His Very Long Ears.*
- Discuss Jackrabbit's listening behavior (page 40, Enjoying the Book, #2).
- Make Jackrabbit's ears (page 41, #7).
- Discover what your children's favorite desert animals are (page 40, #3).
- Play "Jump the Snake" (page 69).

Lesson 2

- Reread the story. Have your children join in the re-telling using stick puppets (page 40, #4).

- Recite the poem "Jackrabbit's Ears" (page 46).
- Create animal necklaces (page 41, #1).
- Complete the coloring sheet (page 41, #2).

Lesson 3

- Review the story and have your children act out the physical actions the animals make when moving (page 40, #5).
- Discuss shadows (page 41, #5).
- Prepare to complete your Native-American unit by planning for a powwow (page 74).

Overview of Activities

Setting the Stage

1. Make animal-track reliefs. Near your schoolyard, find some animal tracks made by a dog, cat, or other native fauna. Mix a small batch of plaster of paris and pour a small amount into each track print; allow to dry. Lift up the dried plaster cast, brush off any excess dirt, and you will see a negative track print. Display the track prints in your classroom for all to touch and feel. To conclude this activity, have the children complete the matching-tracks activity (page 64).

2. Decorate your room with some native desert plants (cacti, yuccas, succulents, etc.). Show these plants to the children and explain that the book you are about to read is about animals that live in the desert where these types of plants grow. Explain how it is difficult to obtain water in the desert since it does not rain often. Share that these plants have special parts in them that store water. You may want to conclude the discussion by making and eating "edible" plants—Prickly Pear Cactus Cookies (page 73).

Enjoying the Book

1. Read the story and discuss how Jackrabbit made the other animals feel. Ask the children if anyone has ever said something to them that made them feel sad. Discuss this feeling. Great Spirit made tortoise, bobcat, and roadrunner feel better. Ask the children if there is someone who makes them feel happy. What does this person do or say that makes them feel this way?

2. Jackrabbit was not a good listener. Tell the children that they are going to play a listening game to see if they can be better listeners than him. You will need to gather objects that make a distinct noise that the children can easily recognize (e.g., bell ringing, stapler stapling paper, scissors cutting paper, money jingling, water running, whistle blowing, etc.). Before the game begins, show them each object and allow them to hear the noise that it makes. Have the children then cover their eyes. Make a noise with one of the objects and allow them to guess which object the noise came from. Continue the game until all of the objects have been used.

3. The Great Spirit created the four animals in the story. Give each child a copy of page 42 and allow them to illustrate their favorite desert animal (it doesn't have to be one from the book). Display their drawings.

4. Have the children retell the story using puppets (page 44). Reproduce, color, cut out, and laminate each animal shape. Attach each shape to a craft stick.

5. Teach spatial relationships by having the children act out how each animal in the story moves. Here are some possible moves:

   - Be Jackrabbit and jump over rocks (beanbags) that have been scattered on the floor.

   - Be Roadrunner and flap wings (arms) while running around cacti (brooms).

   - Be Tortoise and walk slowly on all fours under a low branch of a desert bush (desk).

   - Be Bobcat and prowl (walk hunched over and close to ground) beside a boulder (chair).

40

Overview of Activities *(cont.)*

Enjoying the Book *(cont.)*

6. Down the left-hand side of a piece of chart paper, draw pictures of the four animals in the story (jackrabbit, roadrunner, tortoise, bobcat). Discuss the similarities and differences between the animals. Ask the children which animal was their favorite and why. Place a tally mark beside the animal each child chooses. Compare the tallies at the end of the activity. Discuss why one animal may have been chosen more often than another.

7. Reproduce page 43 onto light-brown construction paper or tagboard, one per child. (Have an adult pre-cut the two slits using an Exacto® knife.) The children are to cut out the jackrabbit's head and ears. Then have them carefully slip the ears into the slits from the back side of the jackrabbit's face. Push the ears upward to watch them grow. Eventually, the ears should be taped into place making them the longest they can be without falling out of the slits.

Extending the Book

1. The Zuni people of the Southwest are known for their animal fetish (an object that is supposed to have magical powers) carvings. The carvings were, and still are, made from clay, stones, shells, turquoise, and mother of pearl. One of the most popular ways to wear a fetish is as a necklace. Have your children make their own necklaces (page 45). Reproduce this page onto white construction paper, one per child. Have the children color the animals and cut them out on the dotted lines. Punch a hole at the marked spots with a hole punch. String the animals together on a piece of yarn; wear as a necklace. (If desired, place two to three plastic beads in between each animal as you are stringing the animals onto the yarn.)

2. A popular fetish is the thunderbird. Reproduce page 56, one copy per child, and allow them to practice number-recognition skills. The mythical creature unfolds as the numbered spaces are colored.

3. Read other books about the desert and its animals (bibliography, page 80). Discuss desert habitat and weather. To complete the discussion, have the children put together a Desert Scene Puzzle (page 63).

4. "Draw Me A Story" (pages 47–48) is a real attention-getter. Children will be intrigued throughout the storytelling as they try to figure out what the drawing will finally be.

5. Teach a lesson on shadows. Emphasize how a light source is needed in order to make a shadow. You may want to use an overhead projector as a light source in your classroom and demonstrate this concept. Review what the weather is most often like in the desert: hot; dry; and lots of sunshine, which casts big and little shadows. Have the children then complete the animal-shadow matching activity (page 65).

6. Native-American children of long ago loved to play games just like children do today. Follow the directions on page 69 to play "Jump the Snake."

My Animal

Jackrabbit's Listening Ears

Cut Slit   Cut Slit

Puppets

Zuni Animal Necklace

Poetry

Dance for Rain

Five little Shawnees out on the Plains,
The first one said, "We need some rain."
The second one said, "Let's plant some corn."
The third one said, "But we really need a storm."
The fourth one said, "Let's do a little dance."
The fifth one said, "Stomp those feet and prance."
Clap went the thunder—and the rain came down,
And the five little Shawnees danced all around!

Jackrabbit's Ears

Jackrabbit started out with very short ears.
He didn't listen well, and he caused some tears.
Bobcat was sad 'cause he got a short tail.
Roadrunner was sad 'cause she couldn't fly or sail.
Tortoise was sad 'cause he was so slow.
Great Spirit was sad when he looked down below.
After Great Spirit dried all the little tears,
Jackrabbit's ears grew long, and they've been that way for years.

Out in the Desert

Out in the desert where brightly shines the sun,
Lived mother jackrabbit and her little jackrabbit one.
"Hop!" said the mother.
"I'll hop!" said the one.
And he hopped all day in the hot desert sun.

Out in the desert where the sky is blue,
Lived mother bobcat and her little bobcats two.
"Pounce!" said the mother.
"We'll pounce!" said the two.
And they pounced all day where the sky is blue.

Out in the desert where there is no sea,
Lived mother tortoise and her little tortoises three.
"Hide!" said the mother.
"We'll hide!" said the three.
And they hid all day where there is no sea.

Out in the desert where the eagle soars,
Lived mother roadrunner and her little roadrunners four.
"Run!" said the mother.
"We'll run!" said the four.
And they ran all day where the eagle soars.

Draw Me a Story

Directions for the Storyteller

As you tell the stories "Who's Egg?" and "First Hunt," draw each *italic* direction onto chart paper using a thick, black marker. If appropriate, provide the children with small chalkboards, paper, or dry-erase boards and writing utensils and allow them to be the illustrators during a re-telling of the stories.

Who's Egg?

Once upon a time, two young braves who loved all animals decided to take a trip. (*Draw two small lines at approximately an 80° angle.*)

They got into their canoe and started to paddle. (*Draw a small boat shape to the left of the first shape.*)

First they rowed south to watch the beavers build their dam. (*Start to draw a line from the bottom of the "beak."*) Then they turned west to find the fox's den. (*Continue drawing the line so that the line forms the bottom of the duck.*) The little braves started to get tired from all of the paddling, so they pulled their canoe ashore and sat up on the bank. (*Finish drawing the line with a sharp little curve to form the duck's tail.*)

As they sat and relaxed, they saw something small and round hiding in the grass. It was an oval-shaped egg! But what kind was it? (*Draw a small oval just to the left of the top portion of beak.*)

Suddenly, a bear came out of the woods and frightened the boys. It chased them across a flat, open field. (*Draw a line starting from just above the wing and continue drawing it until it meets the tail.*)

Oh, no, now the young braves were lost! And worse yet, it was getting dark. By the light of the moon, the little braves slowly climbed the mountain. (*Begin to draw a crescent shape over the egg area starting from the flat-back line.*)

As they reached the top of the mountain, they could see their village below. The boys ran the rest of the way home. (*Continue drawing the line over the eye until the line eventually connects to the beak.*)

As they reached camp, one little brave reached into his leather pouch and pulled out the egg. What kind of egg was it?

A duck's egg!

Draw Me a Story *(cont.)*

First Hunt

More than anything in the whole world, Little Fox wanted a feather for his headband. However, young warriors did not get one until they had hunted their first four animals.

His mother told him, "Little Fox, if you would bring back the tail of a rabbit, some hair from a buffalo, a feather from an eagle, and a whisker from a wildcat, you surely would be worthy enough to earn a warriors' feather." (*Draw a diamond for each animal as it is named in an arched shape.*)

Little Fox put on his headband; grabbed his bow and arrow (*Make an arrow, as shown.*); and rode off on his horse, Stardust.

He rode over the mountain and down the other side. (*Start a line at the top of the arrow; draw a curve, as shown.*) As he came around the bend, he startled the rabbit who quickly jumped into his burrow. (*Draw a dot in the center of one diamond.*) He passed a buffalo hiding in the tall grass, rode under a tree where an eagle sat in her nest, and passed a wildcat who quietly ducked back into his den. (*Continue to put a dot in the center of each diamond as you mention each animal.*)

By this time, the sun was high in the sky (*Draw a small dot with a slanted line above it directly over the arrow's points.*) and Little Fox was getting very thirsty. He and Stardust rode down to the cool stream to get a drink before going home. (*Draw a series of rippled lines to form a rattlesnake's rattle.*)

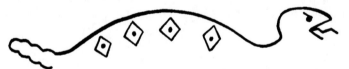

Sadly, Little Fox started the slow trip home. (*Slowly draw a line from the bottom of the rattle back around under the diamonds and up to the bottom of the arrow.*) As he approached the village, Stardust was startled and stepped on something small. He began to whinny. Little Fox jumped off to see what it was. To his surprise, Little Fox found that Stardust had caught his first animal. What was it?

A Snake!

Sign Language

yes

greetings

me, my, I

you

woman

man

night

friend

Sign Language *(cont.)*

sunset

sunrise

horse

tepee

buffalo

trade

arrow

peace

Writing Symbols

woman	girl	man	boy
rabbit	snake	day	night
lightning	rain	trees	mountains
canoe	camp	warrior	days (shows 3)

My Message

What Letter Do I Start With?

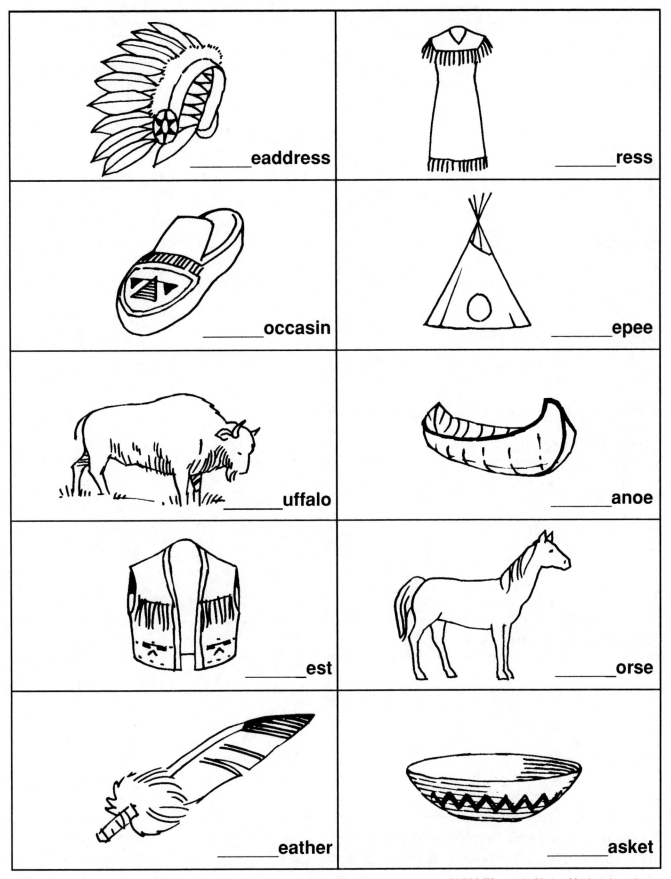

_____eaddress

_____ress

_____occasin

_____epee

_____uffalo

_____anoe

_____est

_____orse

_____eather

_____asket

All About Me

Circle the correct Native-American symbol.

I am a

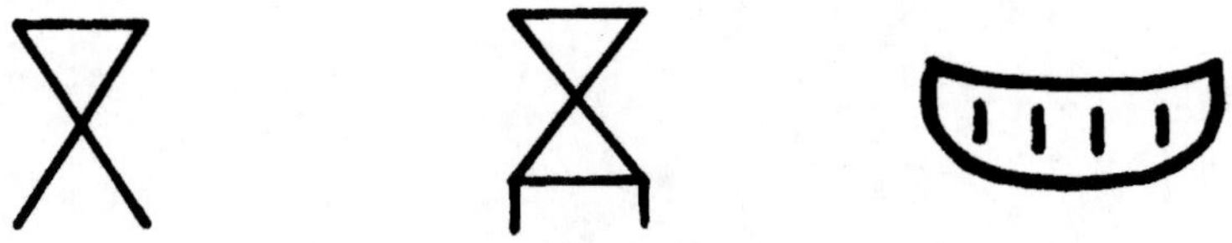

My mom is a

My dad is a

My favorite weather is

Draw a picture in each box using symbols.

My favorite toy is a

My favorite animal is a

For fun, have each family member draw himself or herself on the back side of this paper using the Native-American symbols.

Brave Warrior

Count the number of dots on each headdress. Match to the numbers.

2

6

4

3

1

5

Color Fun

Color the squares.

Blue—1 **Red—2** **Yellow—3**

					1	1	1							
					1	1	1							
						1								
1	1	1	1	1	1		1	1	1	1	1	1	1	1
1	2	2	2	1	2	2	2	2	2	1	2	2	2	1
1	2	3	2	1		2	3	2		1	2	3	2	1
1		2		1		1	2	1		1		2		1
1		1		1		1	1	1		1		1		1
1		1					3					1		1
1					1	3	2	3	1					1
				1	1	3	1	3	1	1				
				1		1		1		1				
				1		1		1		1				
				1		1		1		1				
				1		1		1		1				

Thunderbird

Tall Tepee

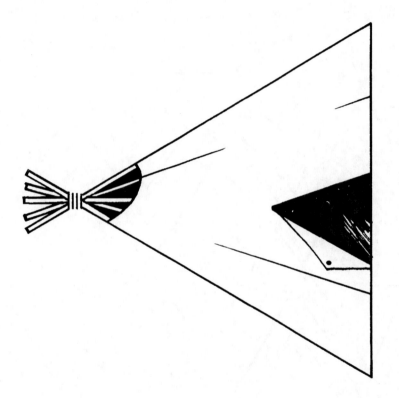

_____ is
taller than a tepee.

_____ is
shorter than a tepee.

Pottery Patterns

Choose two colors. Create a color pattern.

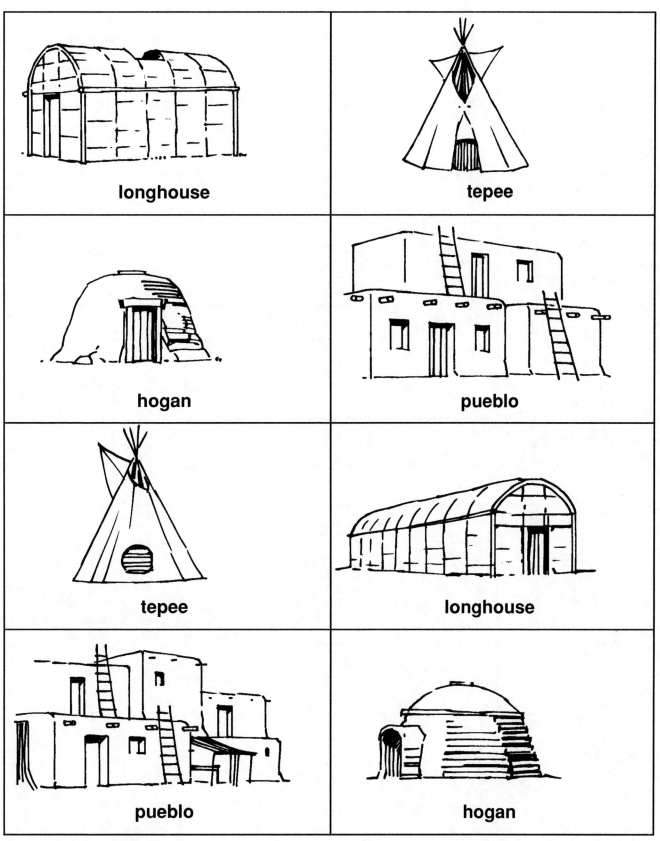

Native American Homes

Match.

longhouse

tepee

hogan

pueblo

tepee

longhouse

pueblo

hogan

Moccasin Match

Circle the matching moccasins.

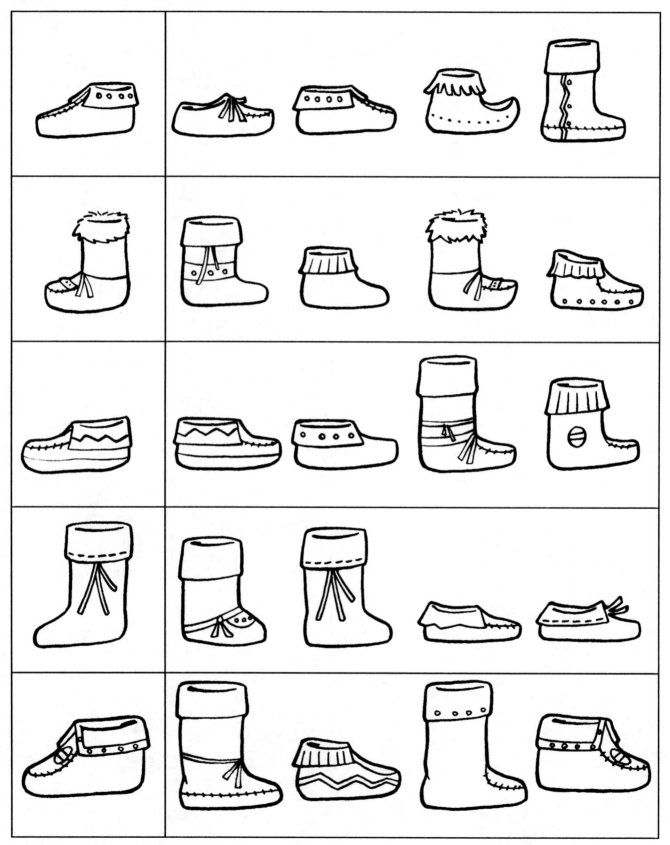

60

Did They Use Me?

Circle the objects that Native Americans used long ago.

Pueblo Dot-To-Dot

62

Desert Scene Puzzle

Animal Tracks

Draw a line matching each animal to its footprints.

roadrunner **bear** **deer** **rabbit** **turtle** **bobcat** **snake**

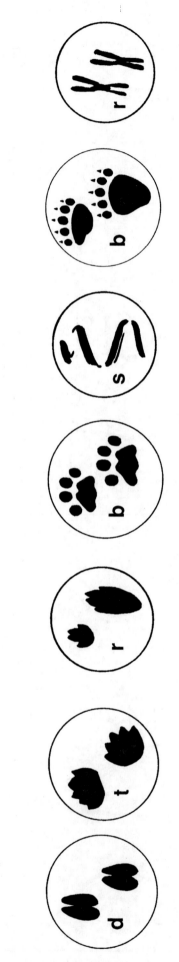

Animal Shadows

Draw a line from each animal to its shadow.

Corn-y Plants

Color the stem green.
Color the soil brown.
Draw an ear of corn at the top of the stem.
Draw two clouds in the sky.
Add some raindrops.

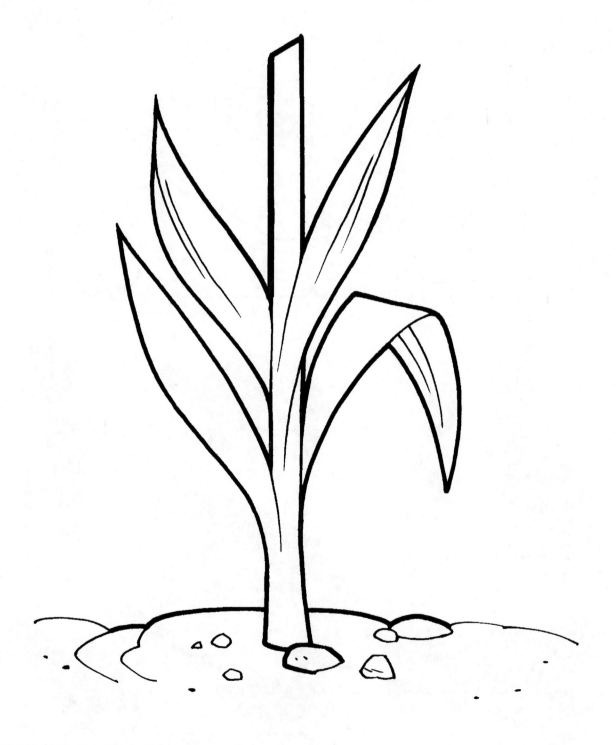

66

Native-American Art

Vest Wear

Materials

- one large, brown, paper grocery bag
- pencil
- crayons
- beads, yarn, macaroni, or other decorations
- scissors
- glue

Directions

1. Open the bag. Draw a neck opening (circle) on the bottom, an arm opening (circle) on each side, and a straight line down the center of your bag.

2. Cut the center line from the bottom to the neck opening and continue to cut out the neck circle. Separately cut out each arm circle.

3. Fringe the bottom edge of the vest by cutting small 3" (8 cm) strips with the scissors. Glue on beads, yarn, and macaroni for added decoration.

Dough Recipe

Materials

- 1 cup (225 g) flour
- 1 cup (225 g) salt
- ½ cup (120 mL) water
- medium-sized bowl
- wooden spoon
- self-sealing plastic bag

Directions

1. Mix the flour, salt, and water together in a medium-sized bowl using a wooden spoon. After initial mixing, finish blending the dough with your hands.

2. Keep prepared dough in a self-sealing plastic bag until ready to use.

Weave a Placemat

Materials

- 9" x 12" (23 cm x 30 cm) piece of white construction paper
- colored paper strips, approximately 1" x 9" (2.54 cm x 23 cm)
- tape or glue
- scissors

Directions

1. Pre-cut slits across the width of the construction paper, approximately 1" (2.54 cm) apart and ½" (1.3 cm) from the side edges.

2. Weave the colored paper strips through the prepared white sheet using an over-under/under-over pattern, alternating the starting points of each strip. Tape or glue strip ends in place. Trim, if necessary.

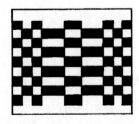

Native-American Songs

Special Homes

(Sung to the tune of "Are You Sleeping?")

Longhouses are special,
They are used for meetings,
For you and me
And our families.

Homes are special,
Homes are different,
For you and me
And our families.

Hogans are so special,
They are used to sleep in,
For you and me
And our families.

(repeat italicized stanza)

Pueblos are so special,
They are made from mud bricks,
For you and me
And our families.

(repeat italicized stanza)

Tepees are so special,
They are moved around a lot,
For you and me
And our families.

(repeat italicized stanza)

Little Star

(Sung to the tune of "Ten Little Indians")

I'm Little Star and I'm sitting in my tepee.
I'm Little Star and I'm sitting in my tepee.
I'm Little Star and I'm sitting in my tepee,
With my family.

I'm the chief and I'm sitting in my tepee.
I'm the chief and I'm sitting in my tepee.
I'm the chief and I'm sitting in my tepee,
With my family.

I'm Little Star and I'm sewing up moccasins . . .
I'm the chief and I'm hunting with my arrow . . .

(Note: Encourage your children to make up their own verses after becoming familiar with the provided ones.)

Weaving a Rug

(Sung to the tune of "So Early in the Morning")

This is the way we sheer the goat,
Sheer the goat, sheer the goat.
This is the way we sheer the goat,
So we can make a rug.

This is the way we wash the wool,
Wash the wool, wash the wool.
This is the way we wash the wool,
So we can make a rug.

This is the way we comb the wool . . .
So we can make a rug.

This is the way we spin the wool . . .
So we can make a rug.

This is the way we weave the rug . . .
It is so beautiful!

Native-American Life

(Sung to the tune of "So Early in the Morning")

This is the way we grind the corn,
Grind the corn, grind the corn.
This is the way we grind the corn,
So we can make our dinner.

This is the way we sew the skins,
Sew the skins, sew the skins.
This is the way we sew the skins,
To make a brand new tepee.

(Note: Encourage your children to make up their own verses after becoming familiar with the provided ones.)

68

Create a Rain Dance

Early Native Americans held ceremonies designed to make certain they would have the food they needed to survive. Rain was essential to the farming tribes for their crops to grow and to the hunting tribes for the health of the animals they hunted. Rain dances were often performed in times of drought. Encourage group participation during this activity.

Directions

1. Have the children stand in one large circle. Ask them to stand very still and be very quiet.

2. Choose a leader. The leader begins rubbing his/her thumb, index, and middle finger together to make "mist."

3. He/she turns toward the person on his/her right, who then begins rubbing his/her thumb and two fingers together.

4. Each child then continues to "pass the mist" until all the children are making mist. The last child passes the mist back to the leader.

5. The leader then changes the motion to rubbing his/her open palms back and forth. He/she "passes the drizzle" to the child on his/her right and so on until all of the children have passed the drizzle.

6. The process continues with passing "rain"—patting thighs; passing a "downpour"—stomping feet.

7. To end the storm, the process is reversed: downpour, rain, drizzle, and mist, until the leader alone is making the mist sound.

Jump the Snake

Materials

- one jump rope

Directions

1. Ask two children to sit on the ground and hold onto the opposite ends of the jump rope.

2. Together, they wiggle the jump rope back and forth to cause it to look like a moving snake.

3. Ask a child or children to try to jump over the "snake." If the snake "bites" a child (touches the rope), that child exchanges places with one of the snake holders and the snake holder joins the other children in trying to jump over the snake.

A Guessing Game

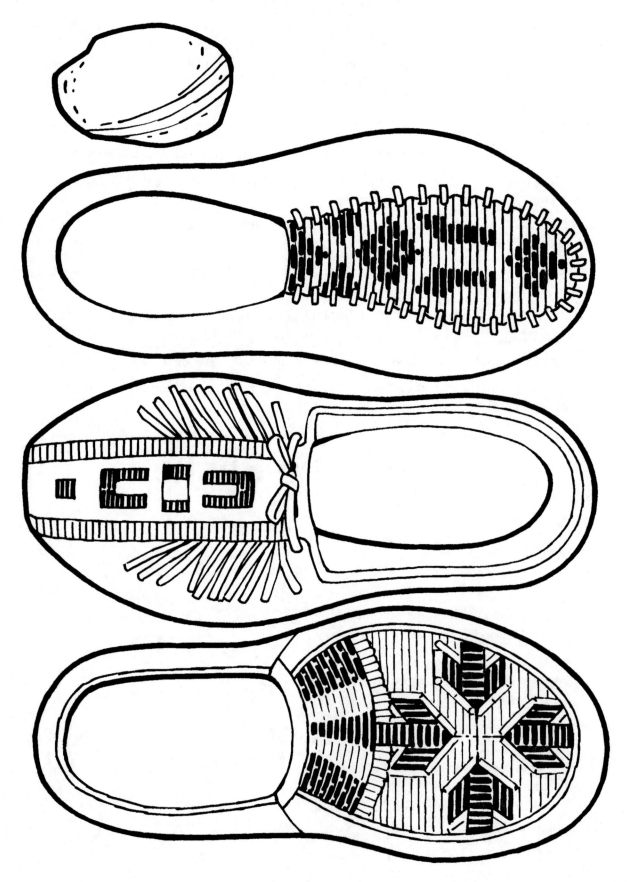

Native-American Games

Stick-in-the-Hoop

Materials

- 3' (90 cm) rope

- 4-10" (10 cm-25 cm) wooden dowels or sticks

Directions

1. Tie the rope ends together to form a hoop.

2. Place the hoop on the ground and walk two paces away from it.

3. With your back to the hoop, toss each of the sticks over your shoulder and towards the hoop.

4. The person who gets the most sticks in the hoop wins that round.

Coup Tag

Counting coup was one way a warrior could prove his bravery. This was accomplished by touching an enemy with a short stick, known as a coup stick. Often, a feather was given for each coup earned.

Materials

- one blindfold
- empty paper-towel tube

Directions

1. Choose one child to sit cross-legged and blindfolded in a designated area in the classroom. This child is given a paper towel tube to hold in one hand (represents a coup stick).

2. The rest of the children form a circle around the warrior child.

3. The chief (teacher) signals for two children from the circle to be a bear and come toward the brave warrior. These children try to sneak up on the warrior and touch him/her on the shoulder.

4. The warrior listens carefully. When he/she hears a bear close by, he/she tries to touch the bear with the coup stick. If he/she succeeds, the warrior asks the bear to go back to its den (the circle) and asks for another bear to come towards him/her. If a bear makes it to the warrior and touches his/her shoulder, that child becomes the warrior. (Note: You can make the game more difficult by simply increasing the number of bears trying to attack the warrior.)

Native-American Treats

Hominy

Ingredients

- 2 15-oz. (425 g) cans hominy, drained
- 1 15-oz. (425 g) can pinto beans, drained
- 1 cup (225 g) cubed ham
- pepper to taste

Directions

1. Combine all of the ingredients in a large saucepan.
2. Heat thoroughly, stirring occasionally.
3. Serve in small paper cups or bowls.

Oneida Corn Soup

Ingredients

- 1 cup (225 g) fresh spinach, torn
- 1 15-oz. (425 g) can whole-kernel corn, drained
- ½ cup (100 g) cooked beef, cut into small pieces
- ½ cup (100 g) long grain rice
- 1 quart (960 mL) water
- salt and pepper to taste

Directions

1. Combine all of the ingredients in a medium-size pot.
2. Simmer until rice is thoroughly cooked, approximately 25–30 minutes.
3. Serve in small paper cups or bowls.

Corn Bread

Ingredients

- 1 cup (225 g) cornmeal
- 1 cup (225 g) flour
- 2 tablespoons (28 g) sugar
- 4 teaspoons (12 g) baking powder
- dash of salt
- 1 cup (240 mL) milk
- 1 tablespoon (15 mL) cooking oil
- 2 eggs
- honey (optional)

Directions

1. Sift the dry ingredients into a small bowl.
2. Add the milk, oil, and eggs; mix well.
3. Pour batter into a greased 9" x 9" (23 cm x 23 cm) baking pan. Bake at 400° F (200° C) for 20 minutes. Place on cooling rack; cool slightly. Cut into small squares and serve on paper plates or napkins. Top the corn bread with a drizzle of honey, if desired.

72

Native-American Treats *(cont.)*

Pumpkin and Corn Dessert

Ingredients

- 1 small, ripe pumpkin
- ½ cup (100 g) whole wheat flour
- 2 ears of corn
- sugar and honey to season

Directions

1. Peel, seed, and slice the pumpkin; discard the rind.
2. Shell the corn and cut off the kernels with a sharp knife. Place the kernels in a pie tin. Place the kernels in a preheated 350° F (180° C) oven for 15 minutes.
3. Add the baked corn to the pumpkin.
4. Add the flour and stir the three ingredients continuously over low heat until the mixture begins to thicken.

Prickly Pear Cactus Cookies

Ingredients

- a tube of refrigerated sugar-cookie dough
- can of pre-made vanilla frosting
- 5-6 drops of green food coloring
- black string licorice, cut into ½" (1.3 cm) lengths

Directions

1. Slice cookie dough into ¼" (.6 cm)-thick circles. Shape each circle into an oval.
2. Bake according to the package directions; cool cookies on a cooling rack.
3. Add the food coloring to the canned frosting. Mix well and frost cookies. (Note: If you want the frosting to appear greener, simply add a few more drops of food coloring and mix in well.)
4. Scatter the licorice pieces over the cookies to resemble the needles on the cactus pads. (Note: If licorice is not readily available, a workable alternative is to sprinkle chocolate sprinkles onto the frosting instead.)

Popcorn Snack

Ingredients

- 1 cup (225 g) popcorn kernels
- 1 cup (240 mL) maple syrup

Directions

1. Pop the corn kernels.
2. Top with maple syrup. Stir until well coated.

Native-American Powwow

The Native Americans of North America have strong feelings about the earth. They felt/feel they have been/are fortunate to share in the bounty of the land. To show their thankfulness and respect for nature, Native Americans held/hold many festivals and celebrations. A powwow was/is one of the most popular social get-togethers. Culminate this unit by having your own powwow.

Preparations and Presentation

1. If you want to invite your children's families, administration, or other classes, reproduce, fill out, and send invitations (page 75).

2. Display the Native-American crafts your children have made.

3. Allow your children to wear their Native-American vests (page 67) and Little Star necklaces (page 24, Enjoying the Book, #6).

4. Have your children show their weaving abilities by making placemats for themselves and also for the guests (page 67).

5. Have the children help prepare some Native-American treats (pages 72–73).

6. You may want to play Native-American music in the background as your guests enter the powwow.

7. Choose a game (pages 69–71) or two to demonstrate or play.

8. Practice one or more of the songs (page 68) and poems (page 46) to perform for the guests.

9. Allow time for each child to introduce his or her caregiver to the class during the celebration.

10. The Native Americans of the Northwest have a festival called a *potlatch*. At this festival, the host shows his or her wealth by giving gifts to their guests. Allow the children to make something (necklace, pottery, etc.) to give to their special guests before they leave the powwow.

Invitation

Welcome Friend!

We have learned about the Native-American cultures of long ago and today. Please plan on attending our celebration powwow.

Date_____

Time_____

Place _____

_____

_____

Welcome Friend!

We have learned about the Native-American cultures of long ago and today. Please plan on attending our celebration powwow.

Date_____

Time_____

Place _____

_____

_____

Native-American Bulletin Boards

Our Message

Create a bulletin board to display the symbolic messages or worksheets your children have created throughout the unit. Fasten two lengths of twine or string to a covered bulletin board to resemble clotheslines. For one example of what can be posted on the clotheslines, after your children have finished writing their bearskin messages (page 8, #5), hang them on the lines using clothespins.

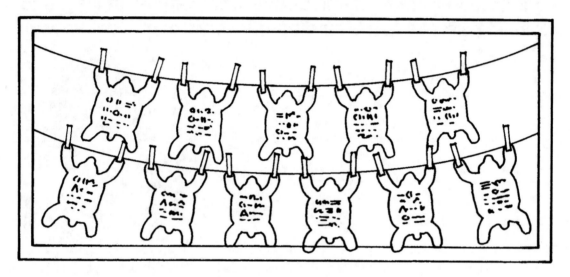

Homes Are Special

This thematic unit includes lessons on the homes of the first Americans. Choose one of the homes discussed (pueblo, tepee, hogan, or longhouse) and create a bulletin board. The example shown below depicts a longhouse of the Woodland people. First, cover the bulletin board with blue paper (sky), then place a second layer of green bulletin-board paper near the bottom third of the board (grass). Make the longhouse out of brown bulletin-board paper; attach it to the background. Have the children tear small light-brown and gray construction-paper pieces to resemble bark. Glue the pieces on the longhouse. For an aesthetic background, ask the children to collect twigs, leaves, moss, etc., and staple these items to the board for a 3-D effect.

Activity Centers

1. Create a tepee reading center by tying five 5' (150 cm) dowels or sticks together near one end with a strong string or rope and setting the dowels up to make a cone shape. Wrap one or two bed sheets around the frame. Pull one section of one bed sheet back to create the door opening. If desired, place a few small rug mats inside the tepee to be used as seats.

2. Make a Native-American dollhouse by using the directions in number one above, only scale down the dowels to a 1' (30 cm) size and wrap the frame with a large dish towel. Provide dolls for the children to play with.

3. Make a puppet stage from a cardboard box that has been cut open (cut off one side section) to create a three-panel frame. Cut a window opening in the center of the middle panel, large enough to permit small puppets to be easily seen by an audience. Provide real animal puppets to go along with the book *How Jackrabbit Got His Very Long Ears* (jackrabbit, roadrunner, bobcat, and tortoise). If hand puppets are unavailable, make stick puppets by duplicating, coloring, cutting out, and laminating the animal figures found on page 44. Glue the paper puppets to craft sticks.

4. Set out a variety of materials for a counting and/or sorting activity. Provide one or more of each object (shells, stones, wool, quills, bones, beads, etc.). An egg carton is a great container for sorting and for storage.

5. Create a hands-on, flannel-board center by creating the basic parts of a corn plant (page 66) out of felt. Make certain that each plant part is cut out separately (roots, stem, and ear). Allow the children to build the felt corn plants on the felt board. If desired, write the appropriate vocabulary words on 3" x 5" (8 cm x 13 cm) index cards (backed with a piece of sandpaper). Encourage the children to label the created corn plant.

6. Set out clay dough (page 67) so that the children can make their own pottery, necklaces, or other Native-American decorations.

7. Provide yarn and colored beads. Have the children create pattern necklaces.

8. Place drums and rasps (page 78) in a corner of your room, along with household-created instruments (such as pots and pans), for your children to create rhythmic music.

Native-American Instruments

Drums

Music and chants play an important role in Native-American life. The drum provides the musical rhythm that accompanies many ceremonial dances and is often joined by rattle and rasp sounds. Some tribes made/make drums from a hollowed log while other tribes used basket drums. The drumheads are most often made from stretched animal hides. Native Americans play drums by tapping on the drumheads with drumsticks.

Materials *(per child)*

- one empty cylindrical container (e.g., coffee cans, oatmeal boxes, salt boxes)
- piece of construction paper that fits the perimeter of the container
- permanent markers or crayons
- glue
- muslin scrap (a bit larger than cylinder's opening)
- heavy-duty rubber band
- one or two small, approximately 6" (15 cm), wooden dowels

Directions

1. Decorate the construction paper with Native-American symbols (page 51). Glue the paper to the cylinder.

2. Cover the drum opening with the muslin. Fasten in place with the rubber band, pulling the muslin down from the sides until it is taut.

3. Use the wooden dowel(s) to play a rhythmic beat.

Rasps

The rasp (a notched stick) is used by many Native-American tribes. To vary the sound of the rasp, sticks were notched in different ways (angles and width of notches). If no authentic rasps are available, make a rasp from a strong piece of corrugated cardboard. Cut out a 6" x 6" (15 cm x 15 cm) square and rub a pencil or small stick over the cardboard's ripples to create a raspy sound.

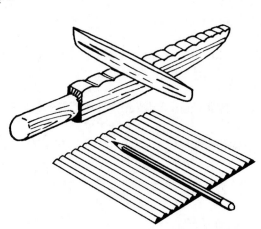

78

Naming Note

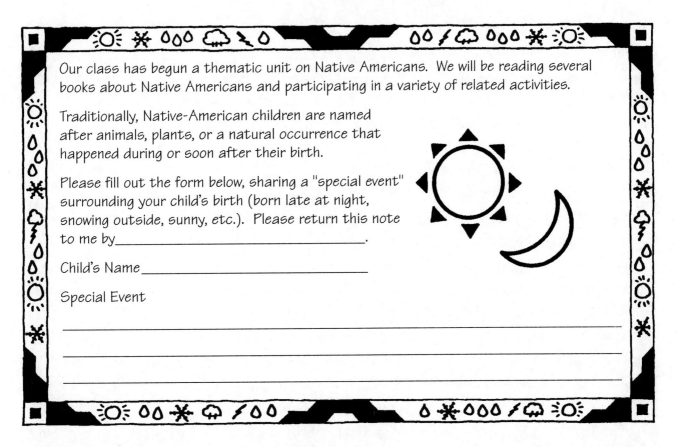

Our class has begun a thematic unit on Native Americans. We will be reading several books about Native Americans and participating in a variety of related activities.

Traditionally, Native-American children are named after animals, plants, or a natural occurrence that happened during or soon after their birth.

Please fill out the form below, sharing a "special event" surrounding your child's birth (born late at night, snowing outside, sunny, etc.). Please return this note to me by_____.

Child's Name_____

Special Event

_____
_____
_____

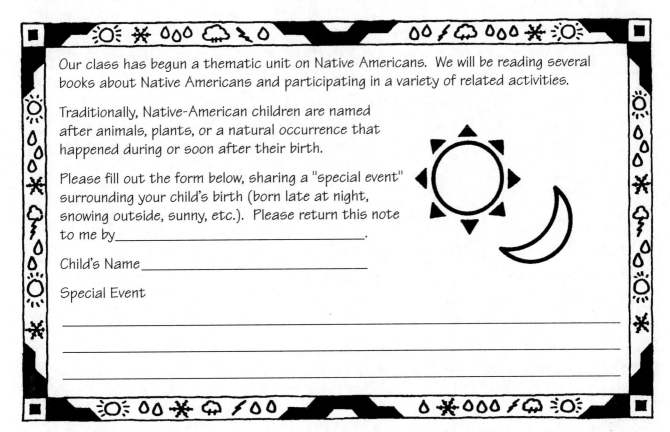

Our class has begun a thematic unit on Native Americans. We will be reading several books about Native Americans and participating in a variety of related activities.

Traditionally, Native-American children are named after animals, plants, or a natural occurrence that happened during or soon after their birth.

Please fill out the form below, sharing a "special event" surrounding your child's birth (born late at night, snowing outside, sunny, etc.). Please return this note to me by_____.

Child's Name_____

Special Event

_____
_____
_____

Bibliography

Aliki. *Corn Is Maize*. HarperCollins, 1976.

Benjamin, Anne. *Young Pocahontas: Indian Princess*. Troll, 1992.

Bruchac, Joseph. *The Earth Under Sky Bear's Feet*. Paper Star, 1998.

Bruchac, Joseph. *The First Strawberries: A Cherokee Story*. Puffin, 1998.

Carlson, Laurie. *More Than Moccasins: A Kid's Activity Guide to Traditional Indian Life*. Chicago Review 1994.

Cohlene, Terri. *Clamshell Boy*. Troll, 1991.

Cohlene, Terri. *Dancing Drum*. Troll, 1991.

Cohlene, Terri. *Little Firefly*. Troll, 1991.

Cohlene, Terri. *Quillworker*. Troll, 1990.

Cohlene, Terri. *Turquoise Boy*. Troll, 1991.

DePaola, Tomie. *The Legend of the Bluebonnet*. Paper Star, 1996.

DePaola, Tomie. *The Legend of the Indian Paintbrush*. Putnam's Sons, 1988.

Grossman, Virginia and Sylvia Long. *Ten Little Rabbits*. Chronicle Books, 1991.

Jeunesse, Gallimard and Ute Fuhr. *Native Americans (First Discovery Book)*. Scholastic, 1998.

Kamma, Anne, Connie Roop, and Kevin Smith. *If You Lived with the Cherokee*. Scholastic, 1998.

Kamma, Anne and Linda Gardner. *If You Lived with the Hopi*. Scholastic, 1999.

Kamma, Anne, Ann McGovern, and Jean Syverud Drew. *If You Lived with the Sioux*. Scholastic, 1992.

Levine, Ellen and Shelley Hehenberger. *If You Lived with the Iroquois*. Scholastic, 1999.

Marsh, T.J., Jennifer Ward, and Kenneth J. Spengler. *Way Out in the Desert*. Rising Moon, 1998.

McDermott, Gerald. *Coyote*. Voyager Picture Books, 1999.

Miller, Jay. *Native Americans*. Children's Press, 1994.

Red Hawk, Richard D. *A, B, C's: The American Indian Way*. Sierra Oaks Publishing Group, 1992.

Roberts, Mary Lou and Lorraine Long. *The Indian's Week*. Periwinkle Park Educational Productions, 1998.

Teacher Created Resources

TCM 276—*Native Americans* Thematic Unit (Primary)

TCM 619—*Native American Arts and Cultures* (Primary)

TCM 677—*Native American Tales and Activities*

TCM 1280—Native-American Stickers

TCM 1771—Native-Americans Bulletin-Board Set

TCM 2522—Kid Pix Activity Kits: Native Americans